Perishing in the Rain

Poems

Also by Toni Thomas:

Chosen	Brick Road Poetry Press
Fast as Lightening	Gribble Press
Walking on Water	Finishing Line Press
Blue Halo	Annalese Press
Ace Raider of the Unfathomable Universe	
	Annalese Press
You'll be Fast as Lightning Coveting my Painted Tail	
	Annalese Press
Hotsy Totsy Ballroom	Annalese Press
Love Adrift in the City of Stars	Annalese Press
In the Pink Arms of the City	Annalese Press
In the Kingdom of Longing	Annalese Press
The Things We Don't Know	Annalese Press
In the Boarding House for Unclaimed Girls	
	Annalese Press
They Became Wing Perfect and Flew	
	Annalese Press
Unburdened Kisses	Annalese Press
Bandits Come and Remove Her Body in the Night	
	Annalese Press
There is This	Annalese Press
Here	Annalese Press
The Smooth White Vanishing	Annalese Press
The Innate Fluency of Roses	
	Annalese Press

Perishing in the Rain

Poems

First published in 2023 by Annalese Press
134 Towngate
Netherthong
Holmfirth
West Yorkshire HD9 3XZ
England

Copyright © 2004 Toni Thomas

All characters and situations appearing in these pages are creatures of the imagination in the service of poetry. Any resemblance to real persons, living or dead, is purely coincidental.

All rights reserved. No part of this publication may be reproduced, stored, or transmitted in any form, or by any means electronic, mechanical or photocopying, recording or otherwise, without the express written permission of the publisher.

Cover design and layout by Peter Wadsworth
Dorelia by Lamplight at Toulouse
by Gwen John

British Library Cataloguing-in-Publication Data
A catalogue record for this book is available on request from the British Library.

ISBN 978-1-7394457-4-4

Acknowledgments

Grateful acknowledgement is made to the editors of the following publications in which some of these poems first appeared (in slightly different versions):

the Aurorean: *"The Sun Bleeds its Spiny Hands"*

Notre Dame Review: *"Five Blocks From Here"*

Contents

Part One *Kitchen Fables*

The Summer of No Rain	3
The Starlight in My Father's Eyes	6
My Father Never Lulled in April	8
My Husband's Hands	9
My Father Says	10
My Mother Resurrects Dead Sisters	11
I Try to Forget You	12
There Are Bad Cards You Can Pick	13
I am Afraid of Cropped Lawns	14
When My Mother Whitewashed the Walls	15
I Run my Hand along the Attic Crib	16
I Squeeze Hope	18

Part Two *The Recipient of Her Own Flames*

My Brother Jessie	23
Jamie M. Always Said	25
When Mary R. Vanished	28
In Mary Jo's Language	30
My Brother's Hands	32
Benign Neglect	34
One Night Mary Ingersoll	35
The Shoes	36
Five Blocks From Here	37

Part Three *We are Gathering Hyssop*

We Rubber Hose Want	43
He Wants Me to Show My Wares	44
I Was Not Waiting on Deliberate Hands	45
It Took Two Dates	46
You Prune Butterfly Bushes	47

The Sick Puppy E-Mails	48
So What if Your Precise Golf Balls	51
We are Gathering Hyssop	52

Part Four *Weeding the Squash Beds*

Failure to Thrive	59
The Nasturtium Multiply	60
I Scrape Dye from My Nails	61
I had Lunch with My Mother Yesterday	62
Tonight You will Peel Off Shorts	63
I Imagine the Night in Love	64
She Knows the Slow Burn	65
I am a Truant Girl	66

Part Five *Dine With Me*

The Soothsayer stirs Tea Leaves	71
After the Dinner at Constantine's	72
Will What We Insist On	73
My Mother Believed St. Jude	74
I Remember the Boy over at Alsea Bay	76
When We Were Hurtling Through Space	77
It is Early July	78
I Follow	79
The Sun Bleeds its Spiny Hands	80
Do all Things Long to Live in Moonlight	81
When I Think of Decency	82

PART ONE
Kitchen Fables

The Summer of No Rain

Tired old soul that's what my father says
when my mother's feet start aching.
She is forty, weary from running miles
across a clothes shop floor
eats fudge marble ice cream late night
after the kitchen's straightened
our lunchboxes stowed away
with their chips, fried baloney sandwiches.

It is the summer I work three jobs
turn seventeen, abstain from meals
try to squeeze my size 14 body into the short skirts
lace camisoles other girls hive in
the certain ones with Saturday night dates
muscular guys who court baseball trophies
perpetual grins
never leak anything of the rain.

My brother ends up in jail that summer
four times on minor charges
every policeman in town knows his radar detector
the amped up insolence of his wheels.
It is the year he paints his bedroom walls black
the smoke of rolled up joints drifts down the hall
but nobody is saying.

It is the summer of no rain
nearly everything dried up in our yard.
My mother's hands are combed cotton
over discontent, gather lost things
coax the honeysuckle up over the porch rail
keep the dogs patient.

In August, my friend Jessie moves to Riverhead
when her daddy gets promoted to manager
of the Stereo Shack, my father loses his job
writes a lot of letters to the editor
stuffs over a hundred job envelopes at the table.

It is the year when strange casualties set in–
my Uncle Amele has a stroke and now
half his body won't listen
Mrs. Slockhum's three cats are poisoned
and a swastika gets chalked on her gate
Mary Lou's mother is diagnosed with breast cancer.
My mama has me bring over tins of meatloaf
every Wednesday.

It is the summer my mother starts gaining weight
stows away her low cut dresses, silk stockings
begins courting polyester, the no iron ease
way it never wrinkles, turns insolent in the rain.

It is the lunar year of the Rat
my mother has not yet shot herself
to heaven on shaven wings
my brother keeps holed up in his room
she goes out late night to buy him pepperoni pizza
my father sulks, is a short fuse.
I pin autumn to my chest
sketch pictures of trees without leaves
the desolate sound of the wind throbbing

end up on an exchange program in England
stay several years
press my face to books with angels and crows
let them speak –
a mute bird on a hackneyed clothesline

from long distance watch my brother
hurl through space
with a truckload of kryptonite towing.
My mother dies.
The men in my family turn into a season
of aimless bats swiping.

I know that to eat the world up
is to court greed
my mother had fiery feet
hands full of deliverance
that she was axe handled from this life
with none of her deftest fruit burning
know my penchant for fallenness
my body's once religion of cake batter.

Sometimes I drink up the rain.
Everything in the yard needs moisture
paths so sodden you can trek
your boots through
splash in the dark
come June
coax a hydrant of fireweed.

Tell myself –
if I can't conquer heaven
the world's shrew tongue
at least I can make myself
a willing wet grave here.

The Starlight in My Father's Eyes

is not for me
fallen child
girl of the Icarus tree
but for another woman
rapt with April's cloves and willful.
She goes along picking hyacinth
even after he is out of breath.

I tablecloth my love
wrap it in chipotle sausages
glazed potato, shortcake
he can eat with a boy's secular lips.

He is old now
has survived a life that didn't need him
a world of frayed shoes
a dead mother, catholic orphanage
too many moves.

I will worship you till it comes right
I wanted to tell him
but that was years ago
when palsy wore an agreeable face
when angel food was my shortcut to heaven.
We don't talk about these things
what lasts
what gets taken away.

My father's stories are shy as birdcall
crusts of bread
the soiled epistle
too many schools
decency that outlasts the rain.

He lives half a world away
drives his car only in daylight
is the quiet champion
of the battle he has waged
to keep steady
perish his past
come to peace with being almost invisible
amidst our country's century of rain.

My Father Never Lulled in April

let the forsythia pet him
forty years old stuffing job envelopes
at the kitchen table
my brother building dirt mounds
wood ramps
spiking ruts in the back yard.

My mother would come home
do anything to appease them
the busted fuse of my father's voice
that rang like weeping cottonwoods
through the room's damp weight.

I wonder about the color of dissolution
whether happiness can grow on a snaked tree
come to worship dirt
the egalitarian nature of it
the way it buries pride, shame
dead bodies
raises hyacinth
collects our past
in a seedbed of April

embraces me
all my travesties
even in the rain.

My Husband's Hands

are big as monsoons.
With one fail swoop
he can snatch up a fly mid-air.
I keep my distance.
Some things dry up before they burn
not every serial version of happiness
leads to a rapt bed.

My father claims industry saves
I say life is a field of Indian paintbrush
melon ripe as sin
juicy as the mouth's thirst.
Cup moths in my hand
let them go
up in the bedroom
they eat holes in my sweaters
the way I eat holes in my past.
Can god make a paradise
out of moth wings?

If I break through the night
will I enter the day
beyond my hands' leaking
will my past resurrect
as songs my children sing
porch bound, clad in pajamas
fused to the flapping of wings
the garden's shrill peonies
all our hard won expletives
unbent by decay?

My Father Says

we complicate what we bend
better to leave things alone
let them sink or swim by their own volition
as if we are mere victory or defeat
the muscular of our own might.

I proposition the dark
stroke the bones of the dead
moon slumbered in my mother's face
camellias' bright pins
sloshed with April

have eaten everything in this world
but not my past.

My Mother Resurrects Dead Sisters

resurrects the boy dragged under
the ice pond's hard skin
kitten with one eye
old man who died alone
three coops of pigeons in wait
on the roof

my mother
her vestibule of silk
laid underground
pink travesties
that nail phantom sunbeams
to the dirt

my mother
who turns us into acrobats
who must watch, learn diligently
that if we can't sidestep the rain
high wire our past
at least we can drink from it

make ourselves a sopping wet grave.

I Try to Forget You

poke holes in my life
the ground so wet and crumbled
it can hold almost any weak thing
imagine love notes torched with spring
petaled kisses
a sun that never needs to
wanton the sky
set up a weigh scale

nobody dead
flown off to heaven on broken stilts
imagine a grave so soft
rain spattered
the wild iris
lupine rise up
impervious
grateful.

There Are Bad Cards You Can Pick

my only brother holds lots of fives
no queens
pedestrians his days
waits on the night's shrew face.

In the dark
rock travels everywhere
white powder on parched hands.

Unpeel the pages of his life
there is a dead mother
lost boy
four wheeler that ruts out the yard
father with orphaned fists.

I am knitting my brother a scarf
to winter in.
It is an unscarred river
season of careful thread
sturdy as my angry
sad love for him.

I am Afraid of Cropped Lawns

houses with card sharks
thin angled light
bone china and crystal
nights that justify
are a homage to paint.

In April I crimp hems
make room for jagged bread
in my mouth's kitchen
know any girl can vanish
with a rapt flame.

Now the dark is no tyrant.
My damp tongue dines
on every rank thing.

When My Mother Whitewashed the Walls of the Yard Shed

painted giant dahlias, blades of grass
play acted
I was ten, my brother five
and nothing constituted desertion
over her fly- by- night ways
it took ten more years to grow impatient
with my father's hacked voice
her sugar water, flaked mascara
fishnet stockings.

Later, we never said *I want to resurrect
what you've lost*
never truly knew the price of dissolution
in a designer world.

Now when my children idle with me
over another song and dance number
forgive me my chipped octaves
I find myself wondering what
ten years will bring

will they grow sensible
staple the past to a black mount
or hive magic in their wings
outlive the rancor of our grownup ways.

Perhaps July is not even coated
with a smug paintbrush
but oyster laden with
every lost thing.

I Run my Hand Along the Attic Crib

where my son's six pound body once napped
remember our farmhouse rental in the coast range
35 acres of meadow and fir
rows of pattypan squash, tomatoes, spinach
the sun's southern tutelage
snap peas splashed over six foot rails.

When our son was three I moved with him
back to a ground floor apartment in the city
remember the back deck stippled in vines
apples fallen in the yard
how odd strangers would knock at the door
ask polite if they could gather them.
We were poor that winter
I sold my stereo, car, engagement ring
managed to get energy assistance
bicycled to the office where social security holders
came in for their checks, some dying of heroin
others alcohol or ex-Vietnam riddled
worse off by far and yet hauling in an old t.v.
to give me because *your kid needs cartoons*
or once in a while a perfectly fine toaster, coffee pot
somebody had left in a dumpster.
Too young my son went into childcare
visited his dad on weekends out in the Coast Range
made paper planes, sailed them between us
tried valiantly to build a bridge.

My son is almost twelve now
holds a skewered map of the world
is good at dance, cartoons
paints with a deft hand
wants to homeschool for a while

stay home, make things, read books
imagine the world as a welcome meadow.

I know there is something we need to make up
how he yearns to rework the past
into more than his heart's trembling
trust decency
that others will want to see his clay figures
know the stories he carries.

Tell me - is happiness a swinging door
will what we go through come back to us
as the summer's field grass
prospect of wild daisies half fallen
but undeterred by the gate?

I have a boy child.
He may never know amid the
roller coaster of life's push pins
the length of my love.
Every pain he has ever witnessed
is the sodden child's crucible
the catalyst for painting ships
that lurch yet surmount a serpent sea
castles under siege
black and white sketches where a
small boy in a hooded cloak walks away
down a narrow grove of cottonwoods
toward the unknown future
some unpredictable god has
bequeathed for him.

I Squeeze Hope

out of the garden hose
press waistbands of begonia
into a window box
have decided that my children
have this one life to live
this one sojourn playing with marbles
climbing the trellises that lead
to the madness of roses

have taken them out of school
that chorus of straight benchmarks
dwindling art
let them climb the elbow of trees
listen to nightfall
the frogs mouthing their lust
into the neighbor's back yard.

They say water will heal any thirst
turn a man less sulky.
I hose the brick path, lettuce starts
my woman sculptures
hose the children's bare toes
the picture of my husband
holding up the world
with the weight of his fists.

If I become the color yellow
an emblem that sees magic
into the shreds of the day
scent my skin hickory
the forgotten enunciations
will the world look back
more than provisional

marvel at the field of spring onion
red clover I have laid?
Will my silk purse come back
beaded in mother of pearl
a rarer kind of filigree?

PART TWO

The Recipient of Her Own Flames

My Brother Jessie

chews more than he eats
it's been like that
ever since his wads of gum
the world's quick talk set in
pool tables with too many holes
cheeky women who light up his smokes
shoot mean ball, want his money
some of his moonlight.
But they won't have it
not with my brother
he has never married
has no kids
stays arm's length
keeps a sad hole in his heart
where my dead mother lives
smokes it, snorts it, sinks it into his arms
and it never talks back
not like the factory foreman
'87 Chevy exhaust system
my father with his whiplash words.

I empty his trash cans
reel in dead sneakers
watch my brother pile up bills
do well at his job for a year or two
then wander away.

If a cat has nine lives
my brother is on the seventh one.
Even the ambulance driver last weekend
must have smelled the angel of death
perched over his head
convoluted body
when that kidney stone
nailed him and he thought

it was an overdose
told the friend shooting up with him
let me die on the living room floor.
She didn't listen, called an ambulance instead.

I have not made out an obituary
but when the boughs of April bend
into the azalea's mauve flame
when the iris splay their delicate petals
open to the wind's loose tongue
I think of you Jessie
think of my mother rowing you away
to heaven on shrunken knees
the flush of the river glad finally
to receive your body
your worn shoes washed in silt
all the waters beyond Babylon
carrying you home.

Jamie M. Always Said

she was going out in style.
I was never sure what that meant
except for hot dates with Joe W.
who longed with his slicked back hair
to be the James Dean of our high school
but never was.

Jamie dropped out of school freshman year
at the state university
my aunt told me she was having troubles
and left it at that
we all thought boy trouble
remembered her short skirts, pierced nose
pregnant maybe with somebody's kid
rumor was she'd already had one abortion
the summer we turned seventeen.

Nelson, Oregon may not be the most
forgiving town on the earth
people tend to hold grudges.
Some of the old ladies have big ears
church clutching purse strings
never really forgave Jamie's mom for wasting her life
marrying a man who hightailed it out of town
with another woman, left her to raise two kids
on a motel paycheck.

I could paint my toenails fire engine red here
trade gossip, eat pasta and grow fat
live my adult life in a cluttered bungalow
with some tobacco spitting man
a shit load of kids crammed into a pickup

singing hallelujah praises
up and down the dusty road.

But Jamie was always the girl with quick feet
a mind that didn't get cramped up.
I remember one Sunday when she was ten
she sat on the church steps for two hours
before her mother's sobs, shaky resolutions
gave way to the minister's bell calling.
But the church sermons never did seem
to catch up with Jamie.

Merriweather Johnson will live a long life
with slate shoes that slide over everywhere
skim hostile surfaces
make ice ponds out of the rain.
Jamie used to say that
it was one of her made up people
somebody who swept into our lives
one February and stayed.
She liked reminding us what Merriweather
would do when the trawler sank that frigid Christmas
in 1996 off Burdock Point, the way her arms
like steel pivots would swoop up survivors
how Merriweather wanders barefoot into spring
wears her deftly hemmed chiffon into the plowed places
makes the crops grow twice as high
come August thanks to her flirt.

So it was not without remorse
that my mother's sister told me
the real truth about Jamie's fall from grace.
It was mid-November
she had a truck load of homework, mid-term exams.
Her mother was being troubled with some lodger

always calling on the dorm phone
and the younger brother kept threatening to run away.
Money was tight
Jamie worked at the Thriftway on weekends
shelved books in the campus library
two afternoons a week.
Something snapped, nobody knows what
she started missing classes
hiding away in the closet of her room.
A dorm mate told me she's down to 89 pounds
we'd never recognize her.
That the rest of the term
she only drank bottles of water
at the bathroom tap, stepped into
the campus cafeteria on Sundays
sat and ate one scrambled egg.

I think of Miss Merriweather
what she'd do in dire circumstances
would she plant purple tomatoes
improve on the mineral content of water
skate over every ruptured pond, crass word
exit the world not with her wrists bleeding
but piquant
snow coated even
seal skinned
smelling of winter
slide over every dire thing
till she was gone?

When Mary R. Vanished

from the Rosemore Detention Center
nobody spent more than a few weeks
tracking down leads.
She was sixteen, overweight
not pretty like other missing girls
the slim blonde ones we see on t.v.
had a history of family abuse
foster placements.
The director suspected she was
on her way to California where
a half-brother lived
left a message alerting him
never heard back.

When my mother stepped off the curb
shot her body toward heaven
nobody informed the newspapers
made a public spectacle
her death was as small as some people
would say her life was -
Shirley Marie Clare dead of heart failure
misdiagnosis, leaves behind
her husband, Richard, two kids.
But I know better
know that under anonymous surfaces
strange things stew.

When the sculptor, George Mendelstrobe
said at the age of 87 that his life had been
a series of disasters
that any harsh wind might have ruined him

I found myself thinking of Mary R.
fortune's undependable coat sleeves
my mother with her clotheslined yard
the way oblivion can starve
the stranded bird
set up a death sentence
or meager tent
where even scraps of sun
attempt to stay precious.

In Mary Jo's Language

nothing is the summer of kisses
no one gets to walk over the surface
of the moon without their feet bleeding.
I buy her Reese's bars at the store
orange envelopes of happiness that
litter dark suns onto the table.

Mary Jo nails serious-faced icons above her bed
believes the garden's insects won't speak
offer up the nuptial of honey
will penetrate even the whitest skin
with the sting of their blades.

I tell her we can grow up studded
with roses scented so thick
they defy the sensible
of the world's clotheslines
that even girls with stones in their shoes
have a reason to be here
marry the day.

It is June.
The ice cream truck rings
want into the side street.
We tug on our sneakers.
Mary Jo's grown four inches since Christmas
looks a giant in her cramped top
shorts turned tight at the crotch line.

I pull heaven out of our bug jar
show Mary Jo its translucent body
sheen of wings.

She says the beetle will die here
die like so many fields falling under
the whip of the concrete
not even new grass
more air holes will save it.

I want to bicycle over to the corner store
load us with candy
benevolent bees
enough hope to conquer the day
make us more than schoolchildren
lined up single file
spinning nothing
into the calamity of our books.

Behind the shed
a hummingbird lands
on the red globe of our yard feeder
laps up sugar water
sip by sip
in easy time to the velocity
of her wings.

My Brother's Hands

are big enough to snatch
the moon's sweet tongue.
He once believed he could move mountains
with the white powder invested in him
is incredulous he has escaped death
so many times.

I am the sister who chronicles pain
knows dissolution
the unsteady language of trapped birds
knows on the wrong night
when the frost gets corrupted by rain
my brother will erase himself
unite with death
rejoin my early departed mother.

I see superman climbing the
white powdered walls to heaven
indestructible with his blue cape
anti-gravity boots, pinched sky

but my brother is not superman
works maintenance in an apartment complex
has lost everything that once offered itself
is too smart for his own good
tells me boredom, the past
are coarse whips
can drag you into a ring of lions
where you will do anything
high wire tricks, back flips

strangle the moon, slug a policeman
to keep the animals from mauling

keep yourself arm's length
from every evil word
harsh bite
good thing
that ever infested you.

Benign Neglect

the Canadian newscaster calls it
says -*we just don't take an interest*
in other people's lives
and I am thinking about
the nature of vanishing
never being noticed
a chalk mark the eraser nixes
with a cavalier hand.

Are there imperceptible beings
that long to breathe through us
ask us to hold their small bodies
up to lamplight with a willing gaze

will our children grow up to reinvent
the indifferent hand that's been cast
in the vestibule of forlorn things
is it a sin to walk away?

One Night Mary Ingersoll

set her house on fire
watched the mattress, rag rugs flame
curtains, lamp shade vanish.
Can twenty years of want
do that to someone
steal the hyacinth from their door?

Mary Ingersoll three blocks down
her moved away kids
years as checker at the take-out
counter of the Quick Mart.

She was dependable, they say
no complaints
came in 8:30 each day
even as clockwork
seldom called in sick
overextended her lunch break.

I think about the ways
we make a pact with death
what Mary Ingersoll
did and didn't learn here
how she departed this life
the recipient of her own flame.

The Shoes

If the shoe doesn't fit burn it
that's what uncle tells me on a day
when my shrunkenness disturbs me.

He had a triple bypass at fifty
locks himself in the garden
nurses red potatoes
the sweet peas till they climb
the height of his fence
nurses only what he can swallow
with an even thirst.

I tell uncle that I have scoffed shoes
a testimony of flies at my door
that the sun turns imposter
sizzles the earth then escapes

do not tell him
I am a pallbearer of the rain
that a graveyard of shoes rest in me
one day I am afraid
all I love will go missing.

Five Blocks From Here

a man committed suicide
with his lost hands.

When my brother and I were in grade school
the sermons of the Immaculate Conception Church
were balls so rock hard
they were destined to breach heaven.
My brother claims I grind my teeth
he can't settle down in the bed next to me
that grinding my teeth wears down
the triumph of baseball stadiums
he carries in his head.

I can see through any corridor
and out past the rain.
I call this X-ray vision
my brother says it's merely a disregard for reality
and my habit of lying a lot.

He tells me the fire the man set
five blocks down
was designed to leave nothing
no trace
that probably his wife and three kids
out at the movie
will be able to live on the insurance income
grow fat for the rest of their days.

I tell him there's a different story
about hope gone hard as golf balls
nights that didn't speak to him

that anyone can momentarily
strike a light on their tongue
want it to flame

that sometimes the world conspires
to swoop us up
gather us in one failed act of devotion
swallow us whole
and we are gone.

PART THREE
We are Gathering Hyssop

We Rubber Hose Want

table tennis our words
as if they are inscrutable
not prone to dust or mold
not so many rubber ducks
in an iced dish.

On the side step lust lurks
seeps into the clothesline
worn shirts, sensible pajamas.
Out of the blue you tell me
you are crazy about my legs
have told me many things
but not this one.
I wonder at the sincerity.

It is Saturday, the children's mac and cheese
storybooks, game hour, bath still ahead
the bedtime they will wrangle to lengthen
with their lilting pleas.

I want to tell you I have stockings
you have never seen
underthings lacy as sin
that hastiness makes the heart
grow taut as a snug purse string.

There is a weight of drudgery
that stockpiles the want of the day
lays up peculiar fantasies
faraway landscapes.
An impudent wind runs away
with my sail.

You Want Me to Show My Wares

personal portfolio
as if I am the chicken slung on a hook
in the grocer's window

want to assess my juiciness
lean mass over fat content
price point.

I tell you - *go to hell*
but you say – *been there, done that*

so we beg to differ
on the nature of conferencing

you with your glass ball
anxious to constrict heaven

me growing razor sharp
in the side room

incredulous
at the exacting terms
provisional trust
you place
in each living thing.

I Was Not Waiting on Deliberate Hands

Things get lost
when the man you love
no longer sees you
when words become
tainted fish in an oil spill.

Your hands
their steel admonition
what gets squandered
that could have been
saved.

There was a girl
dark hair and juniper
larkspur lounging
with the night's lost lips
a queer certainty
of what life
was meant to be here.

It Took Two Dates

to crush my heart
in your hands
easy prey
easy fallout
my Desdemona shoes
red dress hem
wedded to your
hazardous
your hands
that raise char cake
dampen delphinium
erect fences.

Something has infested us
secret as ringworm
every day a stub toed
sabbatical from want
the tightrope of happiness
teasing.

Like a deft politician
you put your confidence
in the weight of
the mind's sharp city
a winning hand of aces.

You Prune Butterfly Bushes

merciless
with your big hands.
It can be hard to live in the shadow
between want and despair
stay married to the
rain's cramped tongue.

I am the only daughter
a servant of wind
it is remarkable how many
busted hyacinth
I have held.

One day will I take this
bee stung ring
other nuptial
make my pact with death
derelict girl
among the nightingales
plum stained sky

will I fold up love notes
crinkle their linear planes
send them as paper missiles
into June's soft teeth

as if nothing and something
can swing on a sacred hinge?

The Sick Puppy E-Mails

#1 Sick Puppy

Your sick puppy hopes for conciliatory words
sweet coos, a majestic climb up steeply grated ravines
waterfront follies, the mysterious M in our lovemaking.
People call, want to get hold of you, we think you are
in the elsewheres, what can we know of the elusive man
in the ragged pocketed linen
the one who defies the laws of gravity
circumnavigates the world daily with his blue hands.
So much wondering depends on the ability of the earth
to hold tight while we slip into the indecency of bath water.
Toss me a line with sweet revelries.

Love,
T.

#2 Sick Puppy

Did my e-mail cross wires like a love song
rubbed away in the sands of time.
Am I waiting on a purple day with yellow iris?
Will you wake up tomorrow infatuated with me, grievous
over the prospect of leaving this bed, will my version of
paradise in the end save you?
Glad to know there are stations of the heart so luxurious
we can enter them, even in a becalmed boat.

Love,
Sick Puppy T. on the mend

#3 Ex-Sick Puppy

Sends you elliptical message, wishes to dine on jam tarts
cozy corners with rotund pillows
careless words that let their zippers down.
I have waited on you with silt in my heels.
Waited on your hands' spidering
the silk webs you weave over my body's soft slate.
It is Friday. Frisky as lemon giraffes set loose
from their carnival cab corners.
Like me they want to wander your terrain
find the place of green meadows feeding.
Listen - happiness is just a hair's breath away.
Me -a purse of pussy willows on a wind fused day.

Love,
Pussy Feel Better

#4 Sick Puppy

Kissing cousin wishes to conquer your chagrin, pry open
the day's vault from its hothouse tomato encumbrances.
It is late May. The field a swollen continent of red clover
indecent as sin, red as a girl's sheer dress
the glass heart I keep on the shelf for you.
Nothing wears me like you do, almost derelict
in your torn pants, flapping shirttail
chanting Rilke elegies years ago
in the holy meadow of our fledgling faith.
Am I a beggar woman, ancient priestess
of consolation with my swollen lamps burning
my hallucinatory version of paradise?
Will what is be enough to always save us?

Love,
T.

#5 Sick Puppy

Miss Lovenet, Miss Lovenet where
are you going with your regalia of hazelnuts
oars lapping want out of the terrestrial blue sea?
Will he come with you? The man with
sugar water wedded to his hands
the hummingbird's reddest orb of glass feeder.
The moon knows that daytime is only the second
cousin to happiness. She wants the stars for her bed.
Incremental landscape. You devour
the bee's nectar with your gated breath.
The disposition of roses never tarries
among the tiresome fence posts.

Will I see you tonight?
Miss Lovenet indelible with
her pale green jumper
strapless shoes floating.

Anxious,
Puppy Lovenet

So What if Your Precise Golf Balls

never spin off course
land on the moon
come August every child worth her salt
revels over the giant gush of tomatoes
sunflowers' unabashed heads.

You whitewash the night's cruel tongue
call me *derelict*
distain my slow pace
refusal to prostrate the grass
tame bugs into a circus

never really found time
to get to know me
don't realize
there isn't anything
we can't impregnate
with the true weight
of our hands.

I try to tell you
all right minded girls
are never a nemesis
to heaven -
they lounge here.

We are Gathering Hyssop

I remember the day
November rouged with the prospect of snow
the windows stapled in plastic
Dylan's baby tooth tucked in a pouch
dangling on a loop of yarn around his neck.

Tied to the apron strings of this love
I imagine I can ignite candles
extinguish any harsh thing
never go missing in the rain.

Back then I didn't speak about perishing
the small mite that turns drain hole
the way we sometimes squander
what we love
make it into a neat fenced yard
white slate, private emails
till even the thistle migrate.

It is Sunday, the hem of my dress
snagged on blackberry vines
the apples in the orchard rotting to death
faster than we can carry them
Dylan clutching his milk biscuit
as he trundles across the field
plops down, gets back up.

I want to capture it all
the afternoon's indolence
the trees turning shock red
beyond the western field's hemlock

you with your back bent
poised in a blue work shirt
a perfect curve over the rows of hyssop
the calm surety of you
dried mud up your pant legs
way your arms sway
weave in and out of the rows
even with a scythe.

It is growing late
the weather turned icy
the dark driving in a stout wind
along with the forecast.
Darling, I want us to be buried in snow
white as the unencumbered days when
your hands first ventured beneath my skirt
and afterwards we recited poems
under a marbled moon.

I have never understood about perishing
love's thrifty
the way a day can lose itself
in the mind's rock field.

We are gathering hyssop
my husband and I and our 3yr old boy
to be dried on racks by the stove's inferno
my hands scratchy, aching
by the time I swoop up Dylan
and hurry him indoors.

I watch from the kitchen window
as you torch the field with your headlamp
slide in and out of the caked ruts

so terribly efficient
watch you harvest what you can't bare
being lost

impervious to the darkness setting in
prospect of snow
what other things
more valuable
can go missing.

PART FOUR
Weeding the Squash Beds

Failure to Thrive

April can be a hard time in the Northwest
the punishing rain
way the sun lures you into cut-offs
then trundles away
your hands staked
to the clouds' erasure.

How many seasons does it take
to trespass sorrow
tack a durable song to
the day's damp face?

Spring waits on crocus
the rain gutted iris
expanse of ivy hacked from
the back fence

the loose tongue that
promises plenty
in a bitten down world.

The Nasturtium Multiply

across our rock ledges
flimsy as girls with slow voices
who anchor the wind to their legs.

It is not difficult to love the world
on a day like this
cup it in a glass globe
that anoints forever
with snow, the ancient art
of petal making.

Later, nightfall will creep in
draw the boats home
drown the river's fitful.

Sleeping river
your only girl child gone upstream
strapped to a raft with no rudder
absence all that the eye can see
the smell of the wind
flutter of dark wings
birds' ambition to give back
their unimpeded song
for us.

I Scrape Dye off My Nails

rust off the house roof
imagine love and loneliness
as two neighboring boughs
on a pear tree

want to wear my worship
stop halting my hips' exuberance
lounge in the wet grass
swollen with summer

want to accept the struggle
of wanting so much
in a love sullied world.

I Had Lunch with My Mother Yesterday

the phantasmagorical diner of small morsels
who says the world is round when it's really flat
says I need to watch the breadsticks
if I'm serious about fitting into that dress
tells me every successful woman has
a sympathetic man towing
cargo of unmitigated kisses.

I ask for more bread
spread butter thick as marmalade
remember the final look of my mother
as her body departed this earth
her shattered blue tea cup
the fact that time detonates
what it can't befriend.

June hoists its legs up like a chaise lounge princess
spawns poppies, iris, squash vines that never
threaten to upset the vertical rungs of heaven.

I eat with my door closed.
Tack the past to blank walls.
Know that what we erase may not save us
that even spoons have a life
beyond placemats
their small silver bowls empty then filling
the gratitude of stirring the first morning tea
mouthing the crème brulee
sorbet with its pink slush

the paucity of the blued lips
more not less
we have learned to lean on.

Tonight You will Peel off Shorts

sleep with no clothes
remember her in the blue camisole
the way the light leaned on her shoulders
a marooned sail
will not dream of her
will not
in a world of soap opera, modern trilogies
she will grow distant as old people
dilapidated shoes.

You insist on staying young
muscular, buoyant
do thirty chin ups, squats by the bed
remember your friends
the ones in thick houses
their messianic hands
mowing and weeding
what will endlessly
come back.

I Imagine the Night in Love

with itself
almost jubilant
the way a woman's stockings
can rustle past loneliness
into the dark's moist lips

imagine the dead man rising up
product of some miracle cure
that removes the rod from his chest
turns his life into a tabernacle.

One day will I wake up
no longer afraid
quenched as a traveler of rivers
guided by your voice's
durable sail?

She Knows the Slow Burn

of August's field grass
the earth's imperfect kisses
waters the phlox, fuchsia

whittles her words
hushes them inside children
grows quiet in order to listen

realizes what she wants, what she gets
might be a mean thing
in a barren heat wave
or something weightier
god throwing her life jackets in the rain

the clear memory of
snow falling.

I am a Truant Girl

an elegant animal
under my cutoffs and tee
but you can't see that.

It is mid-August
the garden holds waist high corn
paws at the sun
the children and I toss petals
into the wade pool.

If I were a serpent
instead of a shy woman
under the tall cedars
I might eat you up
relegate the remains to a bone game
but I am mortal, tenuous
wonder at the trajectory of your ways.

I can mouth organ the moon
into your side street
strip paint, memorize children
remember the why for which I was called
calm the ghosts
know we are more than
the strict anatomy the world clings to
a frenzied phone, erudite words
metal homilies of the dark tapping.

PART FIVE
Dine With Me

The Soothsayer Stirs Tea Leaves

with her complacent spoon
tells me -

*what will become of you
is more than a derailed train
quotient of field burning.
One day you will wake up
in a stranger's bed
convinced it is heaven
marry a barnyard of thistle.*

I squirm in my chair
used to banishment
the lost epistle
glass jars inked molten

stir blue ink into my tea water
iris petals
petulance that makes a girl
stand out naked in the rain.

After the Dinner at Constantine's and the Accursed Salutation of Roses

When five people sat at the table
to discuss Borges
I was rudely absent
not in body but in boldness
the quantifiable leaps that make
language lounge confidently
in thin space.

But that night when I unbuttoned
my blouse for you
it was I who was grateful to let words
the past slip away
find those other idolatries
that shepherd sin
make it safe
we of the midnight branches of
the silent bo tree
my tongue rehearsing its beauty
on your body's swollen limbs.

This other tuition I live by.

Will What We Insist On

come back
winnowed as wheat
succulent as July peaches
will you tell me that anything
less than happiness
is a faulty room
faithless boy calling?

The world stumbles from my hand
tumbles like a glass jar
littered with insects
the holes in the lid
the green moss
not enough
after a day the beetles turn slow
we retract our greed
release them
into the damp grass
let them stagger away

turn the glass jar into a repository
for flour, lima beans
glass beads, remnant string
as if it's not what we capture
but only what we salvage
that saves.

My Mother Believed St. Jude

would save us
stowed away her silk stockings
snap purse, tortoise comb.

There is a saying that warns
never pluck flowers from an
open grave
my garden is a funeral bed of
daisies, lobelia, poppy.

Last week tucked under the eaves
I found two speckled eggs
want to nurse them
as if I can hatch things
stall the boy on the ledge from jumping
deliver to the lonely woman
a breakfast.

My mother's grave will never be
a headland splashed with daisies
her ashes cast out to sea
my brother unable to say her name
without colonizing sorrow.

Sometimes I ride the night's cool breeze
roam the meadow
gather the spirals of fireweed
trim but never cut
all the magnificence of their mortal stems
erect, delicate

imagine my mother's arms
coming back to soothe

my brother with a decent life
able to unplug the rainwater
lodged in his throat
speak again
as if outlasting death
holds its own kind of scenery

nothing lost or plucked clean
without its center burning.

I Remember the Boy over at Alsea Bay

who ten summers ago pulled scores of trout
out of the water with bare hands
night after night filled his boat
till come September he vanished.
No one knows what happened.

I have secretly made a testimony
of death in my bed
let it breathe under the bed sheets
check it out with my flashlight
like a pinhole in the dark
hope and dissolution
wedded to the same thread

know it takes courage to be here
navigate the undercurrents
dark water
lure sun scalded fish
every lost thing
back.

When We Were Hurtling Through Space

in the arms of a cerulean sea
I tell my son as he turns sideways
ponders the word *cerulean*
wants me to carry on, avoid his bedtime.
This is one of the stories we tell
to calm the squalls of children
the man easily jumps over the moon
the boy slips through the crack
in the pond ice but is dragged back
the derelict cat marries the meadow's ice dragon.

I stroke his forehead.
It is 9:40pm, far past his bedtime.
My son doesn't dance on the clock's eyebrow
leans his head into my lap as if the hours
are wheels that spin forever on dust roads
dislikes half-baked endings
knows that hurtling through space is risky business
there are meteors the size of cranes
asteroids with pulverizing sparks
a hero's sword play.

In his heart he holds the lonely boy's journey
must travel the matte black crepe of his spaceship
know so many missions come to little in this world
that sometimes we must nurse
on the Caspian blue of an inconsolable ocean

float then sink, all our deliriums
subject to shark attack, blue algae, mercury
submarines that rescue or rust
our bodies sunk down
dab in the middle of darkness.

It is Early July

hummingbirds swoop
sip the sky's somnolence
my children bamboo screen the yard
in the hope of backyard parties
tiki lamps, barbecued chicken
fire crackers.

They are eleven and eight
have clear eyes
unwilling to break yet
want the world to shine
like a new quarter
any lost spoon we dig up
wipe down
bring back to life
examine softly
under the light's bare blade.

I Follow

the hard shelled
black beetle into the yard
dig up last year's nasturtium
whip maple syrup
into my children's lunch milk

decide maybe nothing can amount
to something in this world
you stomping all over my field
making the corn stalks lift
finger the ragged ends of my hair
defy my husband's lack of faith.

July. Miracles happen.
They happen.

I know better than to cram mystery
onto a scant plate.

The Sun Bleeds its Spiny Hands

over the house's loose paint.
I would give anything to suitcase the moon
make our love rustproof

but August is no mistress of despair
gathers the splayed orange petals of poppy
blue wade pool.

I imagine the density of a man's true breath
hope sent as curve balls in the wind
all our days a valley of roses
thorn pricks so tender
they lick up the rain.

Do all Things Long to Live in Moonlight

with their periled hands?
Nothing makes sense to me anymore
not like two plus two
neatly tied sermons
hopscotch games where
we pocket small stones
snatch lightning bugs out of the air.

I multiply hope
try to find a new equation
spend my days eyelet as cotton
stretched to cover a shrunken hem.

When the ministries of day turn from me
with their fallow eyes
I look to pond water
in whose reflection my body can
always find its shimmer
the moon's embrace
your hydrant of psalm.

When I Think of Decency

it's a July day like this one
the hard pinned knot of winter
unspooled from my hair
stands of timothy beside the lupine
the hammock's concilliatory gaze.

Almost invisible wandering the hour
in my sloped skirt
that paupers heaven into a house
with cooked oats and rolled sleeves
I bake raisin cake
its dark soil of molasses and rum
dusting of powdered snowfall
fluted body cooling on the pine table
till I could almost doubt
those afterlife versions of paradise
the ones that ask us to postpone
what we want

the meadow out back
burning with towers of fireweed
wild geranium
the knowledge that what we've come for
is already here.

Toni Thomas lives in Portland, Oregon. Her poems have been published in Austria, Spain, New Zealand, Canada, England, Scotland, and Australia. In the United States her work has appeared in over fifty literary magazines including *Prairie Schooner, North Dakota Quarterly, Hayden's Ferry Review, the Minnesota Review, Notre Dame Review, Poetry East,* and more. She has been twice nominated for a Pushcart prize, and won several awards. She has published nineteen collections of poetry and four books for children.

Her figurative clay sculptures have been shown in gallery exhibits in Portland and Chicago, displayed in literary magazines, and housed in private collections in the U.S. and England.

Her short documentary *One of Us* was shown at the Trans-ideology: Nostalgia festival in Berlin and at the Museum of
Contemporary Art in Taipei.

Since Toni loves to create and sits buried in reams of poems, manuscripts, clay figures and images….she likes to imagine all of them out in the world swaying wild as the lupine.

tonithomaspoetry.com

www.ingramcontent.com/pod-product-compliance
Lightning Source LLC
Chambersburg PA
CBHW021129080526
44587CB00012B/1194